Journey to Yalta

Journey to Yalta

SARAH KLASSEN

Turnstone Press

Published with the assistance of the Canada Council
and the Manitoba Arts Council.

Turnstone Press
607-100 Arthur Street
Winnipeg, Manitoba
Canada R3B 1H3

This book was printed by Hignell Printing Limited for
Turnstone Press.

Cover illustration and design: David Morrow

Printed and bound in Canada

Some of these poems have been published in *Poetry
Canada Review, The Mennonite Mirror, The New Quarterly,
Contemporary Verse 2, Border Crossings, The Fiddlehead,
Christianity and Literature* and *Pierian Spring*.

Canadian Cataloguing in Publication Data

Klassen, Sarah, 1932-

   Journey to Yalta

   Poems.
   ISBN 0-88801-132-6

I. Title.

PS8571.L37J6 1988   C811'.54   C88-098107-5
PR9199.3.K42J6 1988

for my mother
who first told me
about Yalta

Contents

I. Journey to Yalta

II. Minor Oracles

14

III. Neighbourhood Watch

20

I
Journey to Yalta

Small deaths

Too often my Grandmother buried
her babies. Their spirits slipped from her
hands like startled birds
or wayward angels no one can persuade
to stay.

Before she could call out
or close her thin fingers, their eyes
fell shut. Someone placed them in lace-
lined boxes, pinned pink roses
to the folds of their white sleeves.

Two survived. My mother
and her younger brother left
unfinished quarrels long enough
to consider the stilled lashes
the small white feet
pointing forever to the sky.

Grandmother, grieving
searched all conceivable corners
of her soul
for evidence of unexamined sin.

Grandfather
who always called the doctor
too late, sits upright beside a small coffin
hands splayed on his knees. Mouth tight.
His eyes bright nails that hold together
life and death.

          Year after year
he stares straight past me
facing unafraid
the omniscient eye of God who is merciful.
Who is just.

Origins

Hard to say
how we got talking
on the bus from Sebastopol
past shivering wheatfields
cradled like white lakes
in the folds of Crimean hills
about Felix Manz.

Was it the history professor
or the pastor from Altona
started us rehearsing
who we are. Mennonites

having come a long way
like to return
in herds like lemmings
to places of death.

Frozen forests declared out of bounds
we surround the old oak tree we owned
once. We stretched warm limbs
along its rough-ridged branches, its roots
loved the same rivers we loved. We believed
it would be always summer

always Sunday. On Khortiza Island
we fall to our knees
searching reluctant undergrowth
for evidence of our having been here.
Our fingers trace names
once chiselled deep
in weathered stone.

Hildebrand   Friesen   Regehr

Rare for us to travel
the whole bloody way
back to the cold Limmat River.
Felix Manz in the small boat
bound hand and foot, his heart breaking
free
to watch sunlight dancing
on radiant peaks of ice-topped mountains.

It's where we were born.

Easter
(Barvenkovo, 1918)

Ten days of spring
spent crouched in damp cellars.
Last year's potatoes extend
tentative fingers, fish-belly pale
probing the rank silence. Lean-bellied rats
scuttle obscenely in the shadows.

Each step in the dark street
a nightmare, each voice
a death sentence.
Grandmother wrapped in shawls
coughing her lungs out
at night. Only the children able to see
adventure in the absurd
dislocation.

When they climb up to the sun
it is Easter Sunday. Tulips are out
and yellow irises.

The wet smell of death welcomes them
home. Inside the ravaged rooms
splintered glass everywhere
and a wide gash like a wound
gouging the smooth face of the oak table.

Grandmother weeping, wringing her hands
wondering where is God
whose resurrection they should celebrate
today.

Preparation

Having nothing
more to lose
Grandfather
forged a footstool
three-legged
solid
for the long journey to Yalta.

Hammer blows
driving nails deep
into silence
sandpaper
rasping on wood.

All afternoon
fragments of birdsong
weaving his heart's heaviness
in and out of
soft spring wind.

He didn't speak
to his children
about fear and loss.
Labourers unwilling
to tip their hats to
Ivan Petrovich.
Knives, hoofbeats
imagined and real.

He only told them
it's farther than you think
from Barvenkovo
to the Black Sea.
A long way for your mother
sitting on the hard floor of a cattle car.

Yalta: 1918

        In Yalta
they found the streets swept
clean of blood, guns emptied
and lowered. Faces
grave

        unruffled
as the dark harbour where
unsprung mines still menaced
innocent ships.

        Grandfather
bought unlawful pamphlets
in the street, cataloguing deaths
of aristocrats. Officers and other
gentlemen dismembered

        indiscriminately
torn from their wives
their lives declared abomination
their legs and arms discarded
in the Black Sea.

(He didn't keep the pamphlets.
No need for cumbersome
unnecessary baggage
at future border crossings.)

Spring

In April apple trees beside the stone sanitarium
swell into blossom pink and white. Soft
fragrance floats through the open window
into the white room where
Grandmother sits, her hands not stirring
soup or sorting herbs to dry
for winter.

She breathes bravely
in and out, a slow aching
labour of sheer faith. Mornings the sun
looks in through the window
and Grandfather brings apple blossoms
an eloquent armful, filling the silence
with a rose glow.

Treatment

Grandmother
neither cringed
nor cried out
when Russian doctors collapsed
her left lung.

She never expected
healing
to come easy.

Each evening after sundown
the long needle
forced between ribs, a violation
she accepted. She understood

the need for wounds
and blood.
The complete terror
of descending darkness
lifted
before one can breathe
easy
again.

August, 1918

That summer in Yalta you turn
fifteen, knowing the beautiful queen
and her virgin daughters lie
covered with last year's leaves

in a forbidden forest. Knowing the world
dangles from proud words of men
whose names you can never remember.
In the long line-up for bread

you try to recall the shapes of faces
the voices from Barvenkovo
already fading. Day after day
running up the path to the sanitarium

signalling white through trees
you find your mother
spitting blood again. Shrouded in red-
flecked sheets she slowly approaches

sainthood. Shaping a grave smile
you place white bread
into the outstretched hand
she offers you.

On first stepping into the Black Sea

Naaman would have understood
perfectly
my unwillingness
to offer my body to it.

Vain to compare
these coarse grey stones
with the dazzling sands of Grand Beach.
This black water a violation
after the pristine silver
of Trout Lake. I remind myself

not the clear rivers of Damascus
Abana   Pharpar
but the sluggish Jordan
restored flesh leaving it clean
as a young boy's

and that only
after the seventh immersion.

November, 1918

When Grandmother is strong enough
at last to walk shawl-wrapped
with slow steps
mornings along the promenade
November settles
unrelenting on the misty hills
around Yalta.

Leafless beech trees line the sidewalks
spidery skeletons.
The summer sweetness of mulberries
moves into memory.
She dreams of going home
to Barvenkovo for Christmas.

At Sebastopol battleships loom grey
through fog. Grandfather shivers
inhales sharply
this unexpected imminence.

In the last train
the children press their star-bright faces
against the glass. There is now
nothing to see. It is night.
Clouds cover the moon.

Grandmother closes her eyes.
Her white face lights the corner.
Grandfather leans across to the children
whispers in each ear
Don't speak to your mother
about the battleships.

By the waters

The malignant toxins of Chernobyl
keener than the steel edge
of our sharpest dreams
cleave the earth's belly
in virulent silence.

They surge into the Dnieper River
where our grandfathers swam
naked and cool in the moonlight
spurning currents and the stern
commands of their fathers.

Swimming they dreamed
of watermelon juice dripping
red on their smooth chests
dreamed
of village girls with sun-bright hair.

The poisons float
their fatal wormwood
till all dissolves in the Black Sea. Now
where can we go
for healing.

Museum

Leaving the wet street
we follow the English-speaking guide
through dim rooms. Her words and the wind
sharp as axe blows felling trees.

In this house Chekhov
wrote *The Cherry Orchard*.
Mist glistens on vineyards
huddled against hills.
Rain shatters on stone.

On this piano Rachmaninoff played
while Chaliapin sang. Chekhov
who had T.B. like Grandmother
searched for words
eloquent enough
for the final act.

His sister Marie kept this house.
This desk, these ink bottles
and this relentless rain
beating on glass
were his.

My mother never saw these rooms.
Wind   rain   sun
she spent her time climbing the path
to the sanitarium
carrying in her hand a glass cup
with two gold egg yolks
beaten with a spoon of sugar.

She didn't stop to watch sea gulls
circling fixed points
on dark water, swooping
settling on stones. She was shaping words
she'd whisper   when
entering the white silence
she'd raise the cup to her mother.

Sanctuary

Sanitariums
dot the hills, white lights
gleaming through leafscreens.
When you come close everything is
just as you always imagined. White
beds in screened verandahs, white-clad
nurses, white silence.

The transparent engineer on paid vacation
waits to be cured. Miracles
of glass and steel
springing from frozen ground
shelved until his heart heals.

When you smile and say *Canada*
a light flickers
and holds. You know he harbours hope
against hope. In broken English he says
he's read *Trail of the Sandhill Stag*
and John Donne in translation.
You assume he means *Death
Be Not Proud.*

When you ask about Ossip
Mandelstam's widow, does she live
are her words heard here in Yalta
has she not yet abandoned hope
the engineer's red-haired wife
darts to his side, light and quick
as a deer, fear quivering
softly in her brown eyes.
You can't help staring at her
slender legs, her hands fluttering
innocent as white birds.

In perfect English she says
Glad to have met you.
Good day.

Livadia

I

Overhanging the dark harbour
Livadia gleams
cream-coloured in the morning
sun. The Czar
for whom the palace was built
had no use for it

after all. His own children
who should have picked roses
in sun-flecked gardens, were themselves
delicate flowers unable to outlive
summer. Before the first leaves fell
their laughter turned to blood-
stains on cold slopes
of unfamiliar hills.

      Nowhere
in these cool rooms
can I find remnants of songs
they must have sung
coming home from the beach
from warm salt waves that always
almost swallowed them.

      No echoes
anywhere of dancing feet.

Only the dull shuffling
of shapeless felt shrouds
we are made to wear
over our shoes. Our passage
leaves no mark, no evidence
that we've been here.
When we're gone the floor
behind us gleams.

II

In these rooms Roosevelt
slept. Here
he listened heartsick
to wholesome counsel.

He breathed this gentle air.
There was little time
for the sun, and the beach
was out of season.

In the end there is no evidence
that he took up his bed
and walked, any more here
than in Washington.

Still his hands remained strong
his fingers agile enough
to shape his name
unmistakably
on the white page.

Afterwards they pushed him
in the wheeled chair
for pictures in the park.

When I ask the guide he leads me
to a window, sunlight
streaming through dusty panes.

A plain wood bench
sun-warmed
flecked with beech leaf shadows.

No one sits there now.

III

German soldiers stole
stethoscopes and sunlamps
whole boxes of thermometers
tongue depressors
every X-ray machine.

Having advanced too far
along the path of pure reason
to believe
legends of everlasting youth
they overlooked the small fountain
bubbling up in the courtyard
behind Livadia.

Russian peasants who knew better
kept their peace until
each uniform had fled
or become blood-stained.
When they had dragged the last body
cold and stiff to burial
they washed the red stains
from their hands
ran clear water
over foreheads
into burning throats.

Revived
they returned to the fields.
Here one can see them sun-browned
and smiling
to reveal white teeth.

Yalta: 1945

Clementine
unwilling to leave
London (England
in spite of air raids
was good enough for her)
Sarah
accompanied her father
to Yalta.

Russian
proved too much
for her tongue.
She tried sign language
and vodka. For diversion

a Russian soldier
showed her Sebastopol.
This is a beautiful church he said
and this the sports club.
This square is lovely
in summer.

Sarah
saw only a wilderness
of broken trees
and shell-holes
torn bodies crawling
from shattered eyes
of dead houses.

Nothing seemed wholesome
not even sunlight
filtered through
trees. The dull sea
convulsed with malice.
Waxen gulls fell
screaming from the sky.

Case history

Buried neck-deep in the Black Sea
we tread water. It only takes
quick flicks of the wrist
the languid kick of a foot.

Beside me the bodiless wet
face of the pale woman
who lives four hours
from Yalta
rises, falls on the salt waves.

Turning to the open sea
she speaks low German.
No one can hear us now she says
except God who already knows.

When we turn back to the beach
at last, I have her story
a thin-edged stone
in my gut. Its weight grinds
into memory.

The woman's glistening body
buoyant, pale as the moon
skims the black water.
She reaches the shore
before me.

Saturday night rally

The speaker is on a level with Lenin
who is grey and hewn from stone.
His words fervent as Rex Humbard's
though he speaks Russian
and his gestures are better planned.

The crowd is reverent
or reticent. Hard to tell
whether the words fell on stony ground
or on deaf ears numb with hearing
the good news again
and again. Unwilling to risk

blasphemy of cameras
you focus your eyes on the hills
past the city. Lights begin to flicker
and then the stars.
Their luminous manifestos multiply
spanning the sky. In the glittering sea
you read reflections of the night's knowledge.
It is music made visible.
It is language you have always longed for.

Released
the crowd flows uncontained
into the fragrant street
moist and white with mist. Behind you
Lenin melts quietly into the night.

Pieces

Leaning from balconies
before dinner
we can see segments
of each other. A pair of hands
clasping a concrete wall
a towel-wrapped head
shoulders but no feet.

We call to each other
in all directions
our conversations brief
abstracts of botanical gardens
museums, the small quaint
coffee shop
it was our fortune to find.

Behind closed doors
of the Yalta Hotel
we keep journals.
We arrange and rearrange the path
painted by the amber moon
beech leaves shivering
in moist air, a pair of children
playing in the park.

Fragments
salvaged and trimmed
to endure blizzards
and brilliant skies
of a sun-bleached prairie.

Train: 1929

I hold my breath steady
like everyone else
I want to stop rocking
back and forth.
We are all caught in this rhythm
boxed in like cattle.
I want to jump out and push.
The train is slow.

Slow.
As though there's time to stroll
once more along the rows of pear trees
heavy with fruit.
There's plenty of time
for one more game of lawn croquet
and afterwards a cup of tea
before bed.

Before the doors are forced
open, knives dance in the dark
riders fill the village street
with death, flames pounding
in my brain, my mother's screams
split the long summer evening
spun like a dream across gold decades
fragile as dust.

Who would have thought
that we'd be rocking
scared, helpless as sheep
watching for the gate
for the star that must appear
and disappear

except from old photos
hauled half around the world.
I will lift them out
gently (if anyone should ask)
on long winter evenings
when the train is a black dot
in the distance. Frost
has shrivelled our pear trees.

Married life

Great grandfather was seven years
between wives. A wise God-fearing man they say
who walked upright beside the plough
leaving a straight furrow. Winters he milled wheat

waited uncomplaining for rains in spring
for his sons to sow wild oats
before taking women to wed.
His oldest daughter died in childbirth.

Great grandfather's hair and beard turned white
with flour dust and age, his face weathered
from winds moaning across the steppes.
In the slow ripening of years

he may have grown lonely like Adam
although he walked with God. He may have remembered
Isaac gnashing his teeth in anger
when the lovely morning sun flooded the tent.

In the fulness of time God stepped in.
Her name was Maria just like the first.
She was young and strong and didn't mind his hair
whiter than her father's.

She walked quietly beside him, bore him
eight more sons. Millers and strong farmers
they surround the old man
sitting in honour beside her coffin.

Emigrant

Grandfather refused to believe
the revolution. It can't last
he said citing God
who divides the year
into neat seasons
day into darkness and light.
Who in the end will separate
sheep from goats.

Order will overcome chaos
he assured the fugitives
shivering in damp corners of the cold
cellar, scarcely daring to breathe
until the gunfire died
the hoofbeats faded from the village street.

Eyes shining he reminded them, the righteous
will inherit the land
their enemies vanish like wind-blown smoke.

Grandfather may have forgotten
for the moment old Lazarus
who was meek and just and
never gained an acre of this rich earth.

Crossing the Atlantic to Canada
hands idle for once
Grandfather, a gentle man
refused rage and vain thinking
about the dead. About all those
who vanished like mist into stone-white nothingness.

Each day he observed the turbulent breakers
the unbridled shifting of black clouds
covering sun, moon and stars.
There was no way to escape
the enraged outcry of the wind.

Agenda

Evenings I meet my kin
in rooms overlooking the Assiniboine
River. A coy crescent moon
flickers through elm tree skeletons.
Lights from opposite apartments
shiver on dark water.

The rooms are well-lit and littered
with fragments of white picket fences
the winter flight through Poland
typhoid fever
and a string of stone flour mills
towering over cobbled streets
in Barvenkovo.

We've each brought something.
I a fistful of stories
my mother told me about summer
in Yalta. Hilda offers coffee
unfolds old letters from the dead.

If I listen sharply
past the conversation
I hear the red and white
noise of armies, cries of women
splitting the night, the grinding traffic
below us on Grosvenor Street.

Peter Kornelius Froese
born and buried in a vanished village
somewhere in the Ukraine. We've lost the name
of his first wife. We need evidence
that his twelve sons our grandfathers lived
where we say they lived
completed what we believe.

This is October. We pledge our words
we'll track down each fact faithfully
by April. May at the latest.
Tomorrow we'll rake the last brown leaves
wrap gunny sacks around rose bushes
and brace for winter.

Storm

During the big blizzard
I am setting straight
the turbulent record
of my relatives.

Having brought them as far as
Germany, I find the road
blocked, they are stuck
in the Russian zone.
No amount of shovelling
will get them out.

My arms stiff from lifting
the first heavy snow
I can no longer control
their story. I can't revise
the cold clacking of north-bound trains
barbed wire fences
marking the stark limits
of the mind's endurance.

When the wind finally dies
and the sky breaks open
whiteness blots out the world.

Dazzled by the pure silence
I can barely see
the blurred outline of hounds
and grim guards marching
with guns cocked
on the empty driveway.

November, 1987
(for Cathy and Christa)

I

This accident
has brought you closer
to God
than you've ever been.
It's flung you
with unsparing violence
into his presence
your young bodies shattered
at his feet, your laughter
broken.

II

In the *sistine madonna*
the child nestles in warm curves
of mother arms. There is loveliness
of line and form. Raphael
has surrounded them with the faithful
saints and angels, pure light
shines on their faces.

But this small daughter
and her mother
lie side by side
sightless
their bruised bodies cold
and stiff
not even their fingertips
touching.

III

If it isn't God
who did it, then
who is it?

IV

We will place you in graves
like two seeds
cover you as best we can
with cold earth, this being winter.
Snow will do the rest.
In spring we will bring you
a white stone to hold
both your names
and the warmest words we can imagine:

mother   wife   daughter

weeping we will find the first
spears of grass.
We will plant roses.

V

We hadn't planned to enter
your deaths
in the family book. We reserved space
only for your birthdates
and the pictures you yourself sent
the latest taken

last summer. You wear happiness
in bright colours
like butterflies.

VI

When we're able to think again
of singing
we'll begin not with our lips
but with memories
of our grandmothers
grieving beside small coffins
heads bowed
everyone singing:

> *Herzen die mit uns geweint und gelacht*
> *Augen mit frohem Blick*
> *Liegen entschlummert, o sagt es sanft*
> *Lassen uns Schmerz zurueck.*
>
> *O wann werden wir uns wiedersehn?*

At night the amber moon shone
on small mounds scattered on the steppes.
In the darkness our grandmothers wept
until morning.

Before God brought them to Canada
he forced their clenched fingers
from the stones. It was hard
to move their hearts
rooted in the rich
soil of churchyards.

My mother and the princess

Both had blue eyes
deep as the sky August afternoons
and both suffered in old age
from arthritis
in spite of bathing
in the Black Sea.

The summer my mother walked
in the warm rain
falling on Yalta
Anastasia trailing a white sailor hat
chanting an old song
about swallows
travelled instead to Siberia
where she may or may not
have been murdered.

Both of them showed up later.
My mother in a decent suburb
uncovered her limbs to the sun. In June
flocks of robins and a sudden stubborn breeze
teased the marigolds.

The princess in the Black Forest
raised cats and dogs. She dodged
with stiff grace
warnings of a certain dying
Romanov. She dreamed of Petersburg
and the peasants in Yalta
shouting Easter morning
before sun up
Khristos Voskres.

My mother too grew restless
having lived too long without clapping
her hands and dancing.
She wanted an end to the rain
and the stubborn breeze.
An end to the endless rising
and setting of the sun.

Collector

My mother throws nothing away.
She has fingers fashioned to gather
small hard seed from fruit that's over-ripe
hold it a while in her closed hands
and hide it from the wind.

Everything adheres to her.
Last year's calendars, lacy patterns
for crochet, pineapple and pinwheel
weeks of yellow bulletins
saved from the Brethren church, envelopes
bills were mailed in.
She collects them with her whole heart.

Keeps newspaper pictures of kings
and queens in boxes under her bed.
They are posed smiling from balconies
on wet moors walking their dogs
or waving sadly from a yacht in Yalta.

She tells me she's had to abandon too much
in Russia. Scent of apricot blossoms
in April, the green silk dress her mother made
shade of a twisted oak, rough-branched, rooted
beside rivers. Friends
and the graves of sisters.

The leaving was hushed
and final. Furtive last words, prayers spoken
embracing the train's shadow. She tells me
how full their hearts were of fear
and emptiness, how they breathed
the last thin smoke from the village.
How little they could carry
in their clasped hands.

Legacy

My mother brings me a string of brown beads
a wooden tatting hook, a set of stays
she claims were made from fishbone.
She says her mother stitched them into waistlines.
I don't deny it. This whole dull winter
she empties shelves and corners
of cupboards in the damp basement
in anticipation of death. She flings things
to the wind and fire.

I dread what she's doing, divesting herself
of all heaviness. She grows light
as a feather, unfleshed
her face translucent and so thin
a small wind could float her from me.
Soon she will be sheer
spirit, essence only. And I
weighed down with warm blood, strong bones
my arms grasping enough fragments
to fill the wind's four corners
and even then too many remnants
for the memory to hold or pass on
grudgingly to daughters.

II
Minor Oracles

Stripped and barefoot

There is nothing between Isaiah and the sun.
Nothing shields him from the pointed stones
scattered over heat-clogged streets
in Jerusalem. Around noon he strides past
the temple lined with beggars, stalls
where they sell walnuts and olives.

Isaiah rehearses the oracles
fresh from the mouth of God. Words
for Babylon and Egypt
Jerusalem
spoken slowly over and over.
His lips seem to have healed
but the scars remain
tender. They bear the weight of woes
unwillingly.

Scandalous the people say. Not even sandals
and a scrap of sackcloth.
They are deaf to the whirr of wings.
They don't notice his feet
beautiful beneath the dust and blood.

The jar

The message lost. Scattered
shards mean nothing to them.
Their city stands complete
each roof in place.

Their limbs are whole. Strong
arms wield whips
firm hands lock wood
around my ankles.

But their vision's fractured.
They can't see the line of chained slaves
dragged pleading to Babylon
blood rising in the valley.

They don't feel the Name
searing the ribs of my smashed body
burning my throat. It shoots
between my lips, leaves me

exulting. I see a quiet shining
fill the temple. Clear water
rising in a jar
new from the potter's wheel.

Incarnation

Ezekiel wades knee-deep
through bleached bones.
Marrowless femurs touch shoulder blades
casually, ankle bones
gleaming in the early sun
lean gently against fine hip bones
belonging once to children.

The hills echo the crisp clicking
and clacking around his shins.

It's the smooth gaping skulls
he steers clear of, grimacing
reminders of mortality.

Ezekiel knows no singing
or whistling will make these bones grow
flesh and blood, rise up from the valley floor
leaping and dancing.
Only his walking through them
causes stir. That and the small silk wind
rippling from hills and the sun
sending a shaft of warm light
into the large and small hollows.

Turn, turn

In exile Ezekiel was free
to dream. He was free
standing on the banks of the Kebar River
alone, dreaming. Wheels

for instance, the smooth curve of metal
spheres catching the sun
the complexity of wheels
within wheels, their sleek round genius
for increasing speed.

Four-faced creatures with wings
guarded the wheels
declaring ownership.
Ezekiel heard the whirring
mystery. He envisioned their swift spirits
brighter than glowing coals
their blinding beauty. He understood
the sheer enchantment of wheels.

The wheels moved only
when the winged creatures moved
up   down   to the left   the right.
Above them a circle of sparkling ice
wider than the widest wingspan.

Ezekiel, turning, saw brilliance
more dazzling than steel or ice.
The words he heard by the Kebar River pure
fire and the voice that spoke them beautiful
beyond imagination.

Show business

Ezekiel introduced street theatre
to the exiles. A critical lot
quick to jeer his crude siege
strategies, his amateur escapes.

He always played the lead roles
himself, improvising props
and costumes, styling his own hair
with a sword. He produced

each piece in his tragic repertoire
without exaggeration. Even without stage make-up
and floodlights, the dramatic
messages came through.

One show ran over
a year without intermission.
Ezekiel rarely missed a cue.
When his wife died his critics said

he was not in full control
of emotions. They said
he threatened to rewrite the script
rend his costume

pour ashes on his head. They said
even the best director on earth
could never persuade him now to believe
this show must go on.

Hosea

Clear from the start
she doesn't love you.
She has eyes only for the finest
linen and red wine.
Gold if you can get it for her.
Other men.

She gives you nothing
not even your own children.

You will tear the silver
from her silk neck, the soft white
wool from her back. Plant thorn hedges
across the shady paths she loves
and leave her
naked in forsaken fields.

You'll never take her back
into your arms again
and again with gifts of new grain
and apples, your aching fingers
tender on her lips, your flesh willing
to be broken. Your bewildered heart
listening for her to sing your name.

Amos

At first the voice is nothing
but the end of innocence.
A melodious intrusion
thrust flute-like between you
and clouds clustered soft as wool
on the horizon's thin edge.

For you it is awkward.
Who will believe?
Who will tend the sheep
when you're gone
from the shade of the terebinth tree?

Later
in abandoned fields
the vision enters you
like fire.

Face pressed to the ground
you feel the voice searing
inside you. It's your voice now
speaking down flames that dance and snarl
untamed along city walls

like young lions roaring. A voice
summoning the unveiled
glory of God.

Jonah

You'd think after three days'
damp oblivion of a whale's belly
seaweed wrapping itself around
your head, the water's deep
darkness, sunlight would be welcome
and a warm wind.

You'd be glad to see the city
in sackcloth, the king
brought to his knees. After all
there is a prophet from Galilee
your credentials waterproof
your voice a trumpet
clearly to be reckoned with.

As for the worm
you might have known
it inhabits gardens
born with a taste for tender vines
and a long soft yearning
for the final ecstasy of wings.

Zephania

I can't believe the preacher
would choose this sun-bright perfect June
day for a sermon on judgement. Geraniums
strut scarlet along white fences, emerald leaves
glitter with dew. Under blue skies
our polished cars gleam in the street.

We are at peace. We exchange bright words
between prayers, approve the organ prelude
the yellow roses. I browse through
the morning bulletin. Only three chapters

in the prophet Zephania. Skimming images
of closed fists and fire
blood poured out like dust
loud wails from the fishgate, I grope
in growing panic for words
of mercy. There must be grace here
somewhere, before twelve o'clock.
Before the last anthem signals time
for the benediction.

Haggai

There is no poetry in Haggai.
Heaving stones, pounding them
into place, under cleaving heat
of the sun, climbing the steep slopes
to the cedars, hewing pillars
for our God.

        We dream
coolness of panelled houses
dream of Babylon. We who have known
rivers more beautiful, swifter
than Jordan. We have forgotten
that former glory, bronze pomegranates
cedar altars overlaid with gold
and gold-faced angels, olive wings
outstretched.

         We grow old.
When we drag home sweating
and dust-stained, the prophet
offers promises in prose.

Zecharia

"... who perished between the altar
and the sanctuary." Luke 11: 51

I thought I saw God
riding a red horse toward evening
through the ravine. In a grove of myrtle trees
horse and rider stood still
casting a long shadow.

I kept right on
looking for the misplaced plumbline.
We had finished the foundation
were hoping to move on to walls
tomorrow at the latest.

I thought it was God watching us
at work. The evening sun blazed
behind him.

When I located the plumbline
finally, he said young man
loan me that plumbline
to measure Jerusalem.

I wanted to explain my need
each piece of equipment a godsend
in this godforsaken place.
Thank God I kept my mouth shut,
handed him the plumbline.

He smiled then as the sun
slid behind the horizon
and the sky over the myrtle grove
broke into jubilation.

I heard choirs singing
in the unfinished temple.

The horse glowed like rubies.

patriarchs

have you heard
about Abraham, the old man
asks   (he's got asthma
          his chest heaves
          and falls
          and heaves)

Abraham had faith, he gasps
followed God half-
way around the world
lived in tents
got rich

entertained angels
in the great shade of an oak

the small boy backs away
wide-eyed   afraid
from that day
Abraham has thin white hair
a bent back and
gasps for air

Pharaoh's daughter

I pull you crying from reeds, raise you
in the shade of palm-fringed pyramids
in the midst of chanting priests
and alabaster.

Who would have dreamed
you'd choose to champion
a pack of quarrelsome brickmakers.

You abandon the sacred
river, trail a lonely god
who gives you burning bushes
endless wasteland.

You tear my heart.

I gave you gold
enough, and slaves.
Enduring promises of Egypt.

Afterthought

There was no room
for infants on my agenda.
Children were not even on my mind
crammed with plans
for temple renovations
and blueprints for arenas
and fear.

My legions had enough to do
subduing stubborn Jews.
Nothing should interfere
with royal schedules, least of all

alien astrologers, loaded with gold
spices and a taste for travel.
I should have sent them packing
not listened to their dreams
and star-talk. I caught something

of their vision, strong sweep
of bright wings. Hosannas
meant for an unknown king.

I caught the reek of rank flesh
and shuddered
as I felt the kingdom reel.

The throne I thought is no place
for the weak. No room in palaces
for indecision. Orders
come easily with experience, and so
the innocents
dark-eyed, laughing
were slaughtered. All

except for one boy
biding his time in the shadow
of pyramids, playing in reeds
beside the river
watching wheat ripen.

No king is perfect
I tell myself. It's not much
consolation.

On the eve of retirement

Now you can finally say it.
This everlasting battle with Baal
leaves you limp as a wilted leaf
from the broom tree
your bones weaker than grass
that's dried, ready for the fire.
You're almost too tired to wash the blood
stains from your hands.

You still cringe at the carnage, the unforgiving
heat, priests crying
on the edge of madness.
And then Jezebel with her unholy zeal
to do you in. Just when you think you see

victory riffling her lax wings. Surely
she'll lift them now and fly
like the young ravens bringing you bread
mornings and evenings near the brook
that always kept a fine moist thread
of possibility. With God

you raised a boy once
from the dead. Hard to believe
you've been reduced to pleading
for a sign. Something
to blow their minds
wide open, while you watch
from Carmel's cool summit.

A wind for instance that cracks
mountains, a thundering eight-point earthquake.
Flames that melt rock.
After a life divided
between the sun's heat and the lethal fire
of sacrifice
is that too much to ask?

reflection

on Stephen's unveiled face
radiance
like the sun's first shining
mornings on the crest
of the lake waves

so unbearably beautiful
so terrifying
the hands tremble
grasping the sharp cold
stones

III
Neighbourhood Watch

Born of a woman

1

You feel like laughing.
From deep in your belly
this child leaps out
from between your white splayed thighs
like a fish, scales glistening
red-flecked and slippery.

Already you've forgotten
the long wait for her
flawless shaping
to outgrow your own
flesh and blood, the sheltering
darkness inside you. Forgotten
the pain that came like the searing
thrust of sharp lances.

2

My sister's pregnancies ended
in breech births. All four of them
wanted the womb's moist warmth
and the silence to go on
holding them.

They reached out with their perfect feet
first, as if testing for warmth, or
trying to find a foothold
in time. My sister pushed them out
screaming
with every ounce of strength.

3

Aunt Emily called to say
Marla gave birth this morning
to twins. Boys. They cried out
in surprise
and breathed, both of them
bravely for whole minutes. Then
as if unwilling to be
small accomplices lured into light
and sound conspiracies
they puffed out their last thin breath
turned resolutely
blue and so silent.

"The readiness is all"

Yes. But you're never sure
waiting in the wings
the words will come on cue.
You can't be certain you've rehearsed them
with the necessary fervour.
You are still too rough-hewn.

Always you resolve to practise
parry and thrust
with a pure heart from now on.
Unbated swords
points invariably poisoned
must not catch you off-guard.

You don't even try to think
the denouement. The immutable
mute tableau of the last act,
slivers of glass and the spilt wine.
You want to keep believing
there's providence in a sparrow's fall.

Dark room

My father shows up first.
The rippled shadow grows a bald head
mouth clamped into smile, his hands
blurred, his forehead furrowed
black and white.

My mother spreads upward
from hands that grip each other
like steel teeth. She's returned
from wherever the lost live.
The magic in this room
can't close the distance in her eyes.

Brother surfaces, showing off.
His mouthful of metal catches the light.
He's poised to escape the gloss
grab a baseball bat
run into the street.

There's sister. She wears her best
t-shirt and tight shoulders.
In this rose glow her chin
trembles a little

like my hands that afternoon.
We had just finished supper
and there was nothing to say.

Undercover

I've rehearsed this
repertoire of faces
poised on my dressing table
waiting to be worn. Each one

precisely fashioned to fit
any occasion in life
or death. Gaunt muzzles of bone
bits of fur laced together
feathers and soft leopard skin
the dry shell of a snake.

I assure you recognition is impossible.
I'll charge out of here
and set them quaking with my roar and rattle
teeth bared like swords, or
glide into a gentle evening
of Brahms and conversation
politely sipping wine
never removing these smooth gloves.

When I return to this room
I'll examine each piece for wear
meticulously join torn parts
with needle and thread
recover each frayed edge.
I must let no one
discover my true skin
my fragile flesh, quick breathing.

If anyone touches
the trembling underneath
I am undone.

Dreaming the moon

Once writing down a dream
I wanted to remember
what you said in spring
the wind breathing joy into your blood

about butterflies.
Something about the way they touch
everything with gentleness
how they hover over hyacinths
light on green leaves
a fluttering of colour.

I couldn't recall your words.
Only the sound of your voice
breaking like a glad surprise
from silence. Something
like the noise of water
from clear mountain brooks
trickling over stones.

My dream was not about brooks
or butterflies. Caught in the undertow
of headstrong currents
we struggled to break free
you and I, from what might have been

an unusually bitter winter
the wind sharp as ice
the sky stone. The cold
seeped deep into our bones
and blood-thick darkness
stamped out the moon.

Freestyle

Skin stretched on the crowd's thunder
and silence. Spiralling
body holds the mind poised
on the violin's high C. Now
in the complete absence of shadows
every thought is visible.
You have wings. Each arching limb
each swift decision of the wrist and shoulder
perfect. Muscles thrust into the music.
Prokofiev. Precision and fire.

You are lifted up, flung into air
spun round and round. A celebration
or an almost flawless sacrifice.
Your certainty, your free unerring grace
cancel breathlessness and cold
fear. Nothing exists now but this. Life
at its most beautiful
and most deadly. The knife-sharp edge
steeled to carve victory in ice. Now
everything is possible.

Moving in

The walls in the woman's latest house
are not to be trusted. Twisting
turning without warning
they withhold doors

and windows from those
wanting to enter or leave.
The long grey corridors
gather together wilfully

to deceive. Her children when they come
will find them shifting
away from the light. The pink amaryllis
and violets are not where she's sure

she left them. Coiled in her bed
she hears the uneasy street
noises. They seep through cracks
in the warped floor. Dust gathers

heavy and thick as memory
in all corners.
She spends hours each evening
sweeping it away.

Missing
(for Candace)

Between pillars of this grey bridge
we look for a torn sleeve, green duffle bag
stuck to ice, part of a leg. We are not
desperate though we cry as we run
the length and breadth of empty streets.

The dog's muzzle is white, his breath gels
against lead skies. We are lost
in December's grim silence, God knows
where we'll find the scent.
Wind blows snow over the trail.
Our bones and hearts ache, our shadows
dance in the mad thrust of headlights.

We are left with fragments, a handful of hair
found in a dead book, a smile frozen in memory.
We lay them out in a warm place
and with the fierce glue of our agony
piece together a whole person, a girl
thirteen and laughing.
She comes when we call her name.

Our tears fall warm and strong
enough to put a face, a voice
to the vision that startles us
night after night
from glittering lights of a star-
crowned Christmas tree.

Cataract

Besides these blood-red roses
I have brought you
a radio. I smuggled it
past clinical conspiracies
concealed in charts
and long white corridors.
Even tangled networks of plastic
tubes could not prevent me.

I am determined to keep you
in touch with the world.
Somewhere in Ethiopia
people are dying. Somewhere
fire swallows whole forests
valleys still smouldering
in spite of rain.

All this may not explain
my fear riding up the elevator
not knowing what to say.
After surgery your eyes bandaged
a white blankness meeting mine.

This radio will sing for you
waves rippling from warm lakes
laughter spilling like rain
on wet grain fields
a skyful of birdsong.

You must tune it right.
Uncontrolled these airwaves
swell with the rage of wind
whipped into storm
or the fierce roar of rivers
tumbling headlong
blindly
from rocks.

Visiting hours

They've been wheeled out from the wards
the day warm and not too sunny
the afternoon patterned by the shifting
contours of blue shadows on grass.

Few can see past the maples where two rivers join
their almost noiseless flow. Grey   opaque
the restless waters move
toward some unseen point. The slack bodies

grow more slack as the afternoon moves on
and no one moves the wheelchairs. Only the old
memories of motion   destination   purpose
stir off and on behind the half-closed eyes.

Could be in that clouded solitude
streams still crest, converge with other streams
catch unexpectedly the sun's last rays
before they merge with blue lakes
or the quiet grandeur of oceans.

meditation

I've taken today's text
where I find it
scattered like flung seeds

on the soft unbroken edge
of the morning
where anything can happen

my thin wheels repeat
litanies of perfect revolutions
over and over

fragments of smashed beer bottles
glazing the pavement
a dead bluejay splayed like a sacrifice

neck bent
its iridescent feathers still
unruffled

dogs from innocent lawns
leap yapping at my ankles then
melt growling into Queen Anne's lace

words can't hold the wideness
of the cobalt sky
stretched like a vibrant benediction

from horizon to horizon
and over the oak trees' emerald
crowns the sun
whose faithful radiance
I'm always tempted to love

Temptation

Let's put a match to these leaves.
It's time to make atonement
for summer's excesses.

We'll send smoke rising
from our suburban sacrifice. This gold
will burn like straw. The wind

will pick up sparks
of our burnt offering
and sweep the stench past Mrs. Roger's nose

and past her rosebush (still one blooming).
It's risky. If one fragment of flame gets out of hand
we've had it. There's a law

against conflagrations of any kind
within city limits. Rituals must be inoffensive
clean. We'll settle for plastic

altars built along back lanes
and wait like everybody else for the third day
of the cycle.

Ode

The angel at my east window can't dance
on the head of the largest pin, not even
to save his life, but how swiftly he transforms
glass from dull to divinely sparkling.

No whirr of wings warned me. My first
cup of coffee interrupted by the celestial scrape
of the unfolded stepladder against stucco.
A fluttering of insight indicates

angels have changed their habits: jeans
and a t-shirt for these upbeat times. And names.
Gabriel's out. This one's Joe, his hair gold
in the early sun, his eyes blue as sky

until a screen snapped into place like a veil
turns them grey. How beautiful in the absence of wings
are the sure movements of his arms. I'm left breathless
afraid that in spite of so much grace he may still fall.

Lilac Street

August and we are sewing parkas
on the third floor of a reclaimed building
on Lilac Street.

                On Lilac Street
children in shorts and t-shirts
balance on the sun-bleached edge
of summer. Their boisterous laughter
drifts past purring Pfaffs
and Elnas poised to sink sharp teeth
into wool and waterproof.

We'll trim our parkas with felt
igloos and Eskimos
wild geese in flight, dark evergreen
forests covered with snow.

The new woman beside me bends
over the bright calico shroud
she is sewing, a ruffled denial
of winter. I tell her
the first frost shrivels our roses.
She smiles unbelieving.
A flood of calico spills from her fingers
filling the room.

                It's hot.
It's not easy to sew straight
seams through all thicknesses.
At evening coyote and black bear
circle our vision. One rare silver fox
slides to the floor littered with felt
scraps, vagrant and glowing like autumn leaves
or like young laughter
the wind scatters carelessly
on Lilac Street.

Neighbourhood watch

A row of holes borders the lawn
each one deep, though the circumference
remains small. Tomorrow
men will plant posts in those holes.

Tonight I dream children
dancing with arms outstretched on the dew-
damp grass. The dance is solemn
and terribly intricate. Quick feet
skim the grass, lips move
noiselessly. Weightless bodies grow
invisible as night falls. Only the eyes
glow, zealous fireflies
etching incandescent messages
on black ground.

Only the careless ones slip into holes.
Outstretched arms save them
from immediate burial. In the morning
I find my suburban paradise
guarded by these wingless
fallen angels
planted like astonished flowers
at perfect intervals. Neither saints nor thieves
breach the implacable challenge
of those bewildered eyes.

Sunday fragments

I watch you chip away March ice
in the grey street
carve thin ditches
through frozen neighbourhoods

as if you could bring us spring
by opening your winter jacket
to the sun   as if anyone could
cancel blizzards by thinking
daffodils and birdsong

or death by planting roses

Nadine in rubber boots
and the white cat ankle-deep
in slush

I flip the record   New York
voices fill the pale space
between winter and spring

And though worms destroy this body

Tomorrow this green crown of thorns
in my window
will open without fanfare
its first small petals
blood-red

Morning flight

At noon the oak trees still
hold in their broken branches
the smashed body of a floatplane.

On the crest of the river bank
wings crumpled like paper, fragments
of the charred tail scattered on grass.

One man dead. Three plucked themselves
from flames, ran screaming to the water.
Staring at the spilled wreckage you are

amazed anyone escaped. A miracle
the English gardens shimmer on the slope
between water and broken trees

unmarred. Delphiniums blue as sky
sun-bright poppies, clouds of babies' breath
fresh now as this morning

when the small Cessna rose from the river
a silver bird in pursuit of the sun.
Its glad heart singing, singing

so full of joy it burst
then fell
from the sky.

November 11

At Oak Hammock the horizon
thickens. The air
fills with geese
swarming like insects from the cold
edge of marsh lakes.
Black lines splitting the sky
with the old call
caught in the wind's teeth.

Shivering
in the icy flatness I watch
the tentative wedges
spearing south.

The pattern wavers
dissolves, the geese
settle squawking on frozen fields.

Not ten feet away
a large Canada goose lies trapped
in ice, neck bent
thin legs splayed
an obscene surrender to winter.

Wings limp, the mate
hunkers in the tallest reeds
in Manitoba. The sign says
the sharp markings on the slender leaves
are Christ's teeth.

Wind bites through my scarf and duffle.

For one moment the sun
slashes through lead clouds.
The earth's cold skin catches fire.
Miles of marsh blaze
with glory.

Incarnation after Hiroshima
(August 6, 1987)

In the silent epicentre
of celebration
the pure in heart perceive clearly
the child. This year
strips of charred skin
hang from thin shoulders
face burned black
and in the outstretched hand
a small white ball of rice
the size of an ornament
one hangs from a tree.

Encounter

"All dying does somebody good."
        —Virginia Stem Owens

The hawk drops from the still blue
morning, hangs for a moment
at the nadir of its arc. There is no sound
no sign of struggle, only a kind of beauty
in the limp softness of the squirrel.
The hawk completes the long parabola.
A point of paradox closed under silk air.

I am left. The only witness
to this necessary death. I will testify
it was no accident
there was ample justification
and some negligence
on the part of the squirrel. I will say
it happened under this brilliant sky
on this mountain which I continue to climb
carefully, poised
listening for the noise of wings.

Translations

Herzen die mit, etc.   Those who share tears
and laughter with us
lie sleeping.
The happiness in their eyes is gone.
We are left with grief.

Oh when shall we see you again?

Khristos Voskres.   Christ is risen.